Countries of the World

The Philippines

by Lucile Davis

Content Consultant:
Laura Q. Del Rosario, Minister Counselor
Jocelyn Batoon-Garcia, Counselor
Embassy of the Philippines

Bridgestone Books
an imprint of Capstone Press
Mankato, Minnesota

Bridgestone Books are published by Capstone Press
818 North Willow Street, Mankato, Minnesota 56001
http://www.capstone-press.com

Library of Congress Cataloging-in-Publication Data
Davis, Lucile.
    The Philippines/by Lucile Davis.
    p. cm.--(Countries of the world)
    Includes bibliographical references (p. 24) and index.
    Summary: Discusses the history, landscape, people, animals,
and culture of the Philippines.
    ISBN 0-7368-0071-9
    1. Philippines—Juvenile literature. [1. Philippines.]
I. Title. II. Series: Countries of the world (Mankato, Minn.)
DS655.D38   1999
959.9—dc21
                                        98-3487
                                          CIP
                                          AC

Editorial Credits
Martha E. Hillman, editor; James Franklin, cover designer and illustrator;
    Sheri Gosewisch, photo researcher

Photo Credits
George Tapan, 20
Jay Ireland and Georgienne E. Bradley, cover, 6, 8, 16
Patrick Nagaishi Lucero, 5 (bottom), 12, 18
Dr. Raul Del Rosario, 14
StockHaus Limited, 5 (top)
Veronica Garbutt, 10

Table of Contents

Fast Facts

Name: Republic of the Philippines

Capital: Manila

Population: More than 76 million

Languages: Filipino, English

Religion: Mostly Roman Catholic

Size: 115,860 square miles
(300,077 square kilometers)
*The Philippines is slightly larger
than the U.S. state of Arizona.*

Crops: Sugarcane, rice, corn

Maps

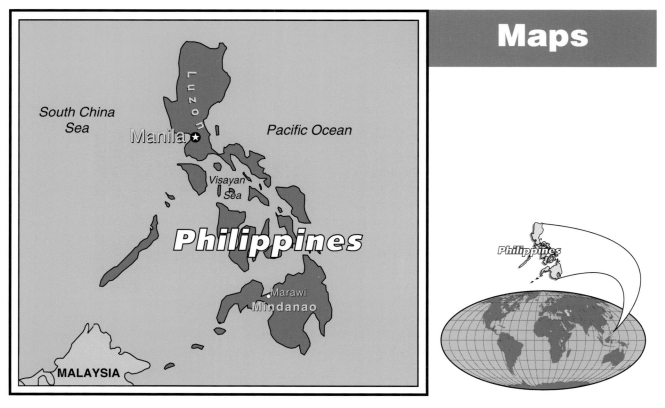

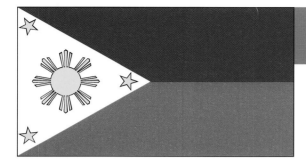

Flag

The blue stripe on the Philippine flag stands for peace. The red stripe stands for bravery. The triangle represents the equality of the Filipino people. The three stars represent the country's three main regions. The eight rays of the flag's sun stand for eight Philippine provinces. A province is a region in a country.

Currency

The unit of currency in the Philippines is the peso. One hundred centavos make up one peso.

In the late 1990s, about 40 pesos equaled one U.S. dollar. About 30 pesos equaled one Canadian dollar.

The Land of the Philippines

The Philippines is a group of islands in the Pacific Ocean. More than 7,000 islands make up the Philippines. Only about 360 are larger than one square mile (2.6 square kilometers).

Volcanos formed the islands long ago. A volcano is a hole in the earth's surface. Melted rock flows out of this hole when a volcano erupts. The rock hardens and forms land. Some volcanos in the Philippines still erupt.

The two largest Philippine islands are Mindanao (MIN-dah-nah-oh) and Luzon (loo-ZOHN). Mindanao is on the south end of the island group. Luzon is on the north end.

The Philippines has two seasons. The dry season lasts from November to April. The wet season is May to October. Typhoons occur during this time. These storms bring powerful winds and heavy rains.

Volcanos formed the Philippines long ago.

Life in the Philippines

About half of Filipinos live in cities. Most live in houses or apartments. Their homes are like homes in North America.

Many Filipinos live in rural areas away from cities and towns. Some Filipinos build their homes out of wood. They make roofs with palm leaves. They build their homes on tall, strong poles. This keeps the homes safe during floods caused by typhoons. Floodwaters flow under the houses instead of through the houses.

Many rural Filipinos are farmers. Filipino farmers grow sugarcane, rice, and corn. They also grow coffee and cacao (kuh-KAW). Chocolate comes from cacao seeds.

Fishers live near the shore. They fish in the morning and in the afternoon. They catch fish in large nets. They sell the fish in markets.

Many Filipinos live in rural areas away from cities.

Going to School

The Philippine government requires children to attend grade school from ages 6 to 12. This education is free.

Many Filipinos go on to four years of high school. Some continue their studies at universities. Students must pay to attend both high school and universities.

Students in Philippine schools learn social studies, math, science, and two languages. One language is Filipino. The other language is English. Both Filipino and English are official languages of the Philippines.

Students attend school from June to March. They have vacation during April and May. These are the hottest months in the Philippines.

Students in Philippine schools learn two languages.

Philippine Food

Most Filipinos eat five times a day. They eat three meals. Many also eat during two snack times. Morning snack time is called segundo almuerzo (seh-GOON-doh al-MWER-zoh). This means second breakfast. Afternoon snack time is called merienda (mehr-ee-EHN-dah).

Rice is the main food in the Philippines. Filipinos eat rice with every meal. Filipinos also eat fish and meat.

Adobo (uh-DOH-boh) is a favorite dish of Filipinos. Adobo is chicken and pork cooked with garlic and soy sauce.

Lechon (LET-chuhn) is another popular meal. Lechon is roasted pig. Filipinos cook a whole pig over an open fire.

Filipinos eat halo-halo (HAH-loh-HAH-loh) for dessert. This dish has dried fruit, custard, and crushed ice mixed together.

Rice is the main food in the Philippines.

Philippine Clothes

Most Philippine clothes look like North American clothes. Most children wear cotton clothes. Cotton clothes help them stay cool. Boys wear jeans and T-shirts. Girls wear cotton skirts and tops.

Some Filipinos wear traditional clothes. Many villages have different styles of traditional clothes. For example, people in the village of Marawi (muh-RAH-wee) wear malongs (MUH-longs). A malong is a cloth tube. People wear them like skirts.

Many Filipinos wear traditional clothes for holidays. A woman may wear a balintawak (bah-LIN-tah-wuk). This is a long dress with puffy sleeves. A man may wear a barong tagalog (BAH-rong TAH-gah-log). This is a shirt made with fiber from pineapple plants.

Many Filipinos wear traditional clothes for holidays.

15

Animals in the Philippines

Many animals are native to the Philippines. Philippine eagles live throughout the country. Philippine cobras are deadly snakes. The tarsier (TAR-see-uhr) is a small Philippine animal related to the monkey. Tarsiers have large eyes.

Monkeys, bats, and wild pigs live in Philippine rain forests. Rain forests are thick woods in warm, rainy places.

Many types of deer make their homes in the Philippines. Midget deer and mouse deer are small. Sambar (SAHM-bahr) deer are large.

Two kinds of buffalo are found in the Philippines. Tamaraus (ta-muh-RAWS) are small, wild buffalo. Water buffalo are large, strong animals. Some farmers use water buffalo to pull their plows. Water buffalo can pull and carry heavy loads.

Tarsiers have large eyes.

Sports in the Philippines

Filipinos enjoy sports. Some popular sports are basketball, baseball, and boxing. Soccer is a popular sport too. Students play these sports at school.

Arnis (ar-NEES) and sipa (SEE-puh) are other sports that Filipinos enjoy. Arnis is a Philippine martial art. A martial art is a style of fighting or self-defense. People practice arnis with sticks. Sipa players stand on either side of a net. They hit a ball over the net. But players must use only their knees and feet.

Every year, Filipino athletes compete in the Philippine National Games. Athletes compete in gymnastics, swimming, volleyball, and polo. Polo players use sticks to hit balls into goals. Most polo players ride horses.

Arnis is a Philippine martial art.

Holidays in the Philippines

Filipinos celebrate two New Year's holidays. They have parties on these special occasions. January 1 is the Philippine New Year. Filipinos also celebrate the Chinese New Year. This holiday is in late January or early February. Filipinos celebrate both holidays with parties and fireworks.

Filipinos make lanterns for Christmas celebrations. They use bamboo plant stems to make lantern frames. Filipinos cover the frames with colored paper. They place a light inside the lantern. Children carry lanterns in Christmas parades.

Each Philippine village has a party called a fiesta (FEE-ess-tuh) once each year. A big parade is part of the fiesta. Filipinos make many foods. They often eat lechon and halo-halo at the fiesta.

Filipinos make lanterns for Christmas celebrations.

Hands on: Make a Paper Lantern

Filipinos make paper lanterns for their Christmas celebration. You can make a paper lantern.

What You Need

One brown paper sack	Tape
Two pieces of white paper	Scissors
Markers or crayons	Flashlight

What You Do

1. Fold the paper sack so it is flat. Cut a hole in the middle of the sack. You should cut through both layers of paper. Unfold and open the sack. The sack now has two windows.
2. Color the white paper with markers or crayons. Make pictures or patterns. They should be about the same size as the windows of the sack.
3. Tape the white paper inside the paper bag. Make sure the pictures show in the windows.
4. Gather the opening of the bag around the top of the flashlight handle. Place tape around the bag and handle. Turn on the flashlight. The light will shine through the white paper.

Learn to Speak Filipino

child	bata	(bah-TAH)
hello	mabuhay	(mah-BOO-hay)
How are you?	Kumusta ka?	(koo-moos-TAH kah)
no	hindi	(hin-DIH)
OK	sige	(SEE-geh)
please	paki	(pah-KEE)
rain	ulan	(oo-LAN)
thank you	salamat	(sa-LAH-mat)
village	baryo	(BAHR-ee-oh)
yes	oo	(oh-OO)

Words to Know

celebrate (SEL-uh-brate)—to do something fun on a special occasion

lantern (LAN-turn)—a lamp

tradition (truh-DISH-uhn)—a practice continued over many years

typhoon (tye-FOON)—a powerful wind and rain storm

volcano (vol-KAY-noh)—a hole in the earth's surface; melted rock flows out of this hole when a volcano erupts.

Read More

Enderlein, Cheryl L. *Christmas in the Philippines.* Christmas around the World. Mankato, Minn.: Hilltop Books, 1998.

Kinkade, Sheila. *Children of the Philippines.* World's Children. Minneapolis: Carolrhoda Books, 1996.

Useful Addresses and Internet Sites

Embassy of the Philippines
1600 Massachusetts Avenue NW
Washington, DC 20036

Embassy of the Philippines
130 Albert Street, Suite 606
Ottawa, Ontario K1P 5G4
Canada

Philippine Civics
http://www.globalserve.net/~studiopi/Flip/Civics.HTML
The Philippine Embassy in Washington
http://www.sequel.net/RPinUS/WDC/

Index